Puffin Books

COOKING IS A GAME YOU

Cooking is the very best game of all : 1
weighing and mixing, chopping, rollir
decorating, and cooking, you can eat

Fay Maschler has collected together some delicious recipes for all
kinds of food ; for cooking indoors and out ; for when you are bored on
a rainy afternoon, and for taking on expeditions. You can make
kebabs and toast marshmallows round a campfire ; discover real
cowboy hash, '1000-year-old' eggs and Gratie Taties ; turn Baked
Beans into something spicey and delicious, and a heap of dry flour
into hot crusty bread. Ice-cream is surprisingly easy to make, and have
you ever eaten Rocky Road ? You can treat someone to breakfast in
bed, make your own edible Christmas decorations and impress your
family and friends with a bowl of exotic sparkling fruit. If you follow
the rules carefully, the results will be delicious.

The clear step-by-step instructions are fully illustrated in black and
white and colour, and they will show you that cooking is not only the
best but one of the easiest games to play.

FAY MASCHLER

Illustrated by Malcolm Bird

Cooking is a Game
You Can Eat

Puffin Books

For Hannah, Alice and Ben

Puffin Books
Penguin Books Ltd,
Harmondsworth, Middlesex, England
Penguin Books Australia Ltd, Ringwood,
Victoria, Australia
Penguin Books Canada Ltd,
41 Steelcase Road West, Markham, Ontario, Canada
Penguin Books (N.Z.) Ltd,
182–190 Wairau Road, Auckland 10, New Zealand

First published 1975

Copyright © Fay Maschler, 1975
Illustrations © Malcolm Bird, 1975

Made and printed in Great Britain by
Richard Clay (The Chaucer Press), Ltd,
Bungay, Suffolk
Set in Monotype Univers Light

Contents

Introduction

Cooking is a game with a special advantage. After you have finished playing – Weighing, Measuring, Mixing, Chopping, Rolling, Shaping, Decorating – you and your family and friends can eat the results. Follow the rules carefully and the results will be delicious.

This book is divided into nine recipe sections. Some recipes are for any day you feel like cooking, or for any day you feel hungry! Others are useful for entertaining friends or laying in supplies for expeditions. And there are cookery ideas for occasions like Guy Fawkes, Christmas and parties.

Things you cook yourself make very good presents. Everyone appreciates something made specially for them – all the more so if it is a bit wonky.

Games are fun. And so is cooking. And best of all, cooking is a game you can eat.

Some Handy Gadgets

Grater	Rolling pin	Measuring spoons
Egg beater	Lemon and orange	Wooden spoon
Sieve	squeezer	

Double boiler: If you don't have one saucepan that sits comfortably in another (a double boiler) you can make one by finding a bowl that will fit into a saucepan without the bottom of the bowl touching the saucepan. The water you put underneath should not reach the level of the bowl or top saucepan.

A Few Bits of Useful Advice

Do (please) always:

1. Before you start cooking get yourself ready. Wrap yourself in an apron and wash your hands.
2. Read your chosen recipe right the way through before beginning. Assemble all the ingredients and utensils you will need and you won't be caught sticky handed.
3. Check if the oven will be needed. If so turn it on before you begin the recipe and by the time you are ready to cook the food it will have reached the correct temperature. Ask an adult to help light a non-automatic gas oven. Remember that the top shelf in the oven is hotter than the bottom one. Use the middle shelf of the oven, unless the recipe tells you otherwise.
4. Wash up. It is a less thrilling game, but worth doing to preserve good relations. Wash up as you go along, and it won't get on top of you.

Don't (please):

1. Start a cooking game just before a meal (unless it is one you are making!) or when the kitchen is about to be used by your mother.
2. Open the oven door when cakes, pastries or soufflés are cooking. Sudden gusts of cool air can flatten your baking.
3. Remove dishes from a hot oven without wearing oven gloves, or using a thick, thick cloth.
4. Make sweets, which involve boiling sugar and water, without an adult around to give you a hand.

Measurements and Measuring

Some recipes measure ingredients in ounces, others in spoons. If you are lucky enough to have a set of scales then it is easy and rather satisfying to measure things that way. Otherwise you can work out ounces in terms of tablespoons. A tablespoon here means a level tablespoon. This also applies to teaspoons and dessertspoons. To make sure you have accurate measurements, heap the spoon with whatever you are measuring and level off with the side of a knife.

1 ounce flour = 25 gms = 3 level tablespoons
1 ounce grated cheese = 25 gms = 4 level tablespoons
1 ounce butter, margarine or fat = 25 gms = 2 level tablespoons
1 ounce currants, raisins = 25 gms = 2 level tablespoons
1 ounce sugar = 25 gms = 2 level tablespoons
1 ounce icing sugar = 25 gms = 3 level tablespoons
1 ounce rice = 25 gms = $1\frac{1}{2}$ level tablespoons

2 teaspoons = 1 dessertspoon
2 dessertspoons = 1 tablespoon

Syrup and treacle: to measure syrup, warm a tablespoon in very hot water. Dry it and spoon the syrup from the tin. It will run off cleanly. 1 tablespoon of syrup is approximately $1\frac{1}{2}$ ounces (40 gms).

A *pinch* of salt or pepper or herbs is the amount you pinch between your thumb and first finger.

To grease a baking tin or to oil foil: Put a tiny piece of butter, margarine, or a few drops of cooking oil on some kitchen paper. Rub the paper round the baking tin or over the foil until it is lightly greased all over. It should just shine with grease, no more.

To break an egg: To break an egg, tap it quite firmly on the side of a cup to make a crack in the middle. Separate the two halves and pour the egg into the cup before using. This way you can easily remove pieces of stray shell (using one of the half egg shells) and also make sure of the egg's freshness.

To separate an egg: Have two small bowls or cups ready. Crack the egg over one of them and *carefully* tip the yolk from one half of the shell to the other. The white will plop into the bowl below. Put the yolk into the other bowl. Add whichever half you need to your mixture *or*

If that sounds too tricky, break the egg into a saucer, up-end a small cup over the yolk and pour off the white *or*

Use an egg separator if you have one.

To chop an onion: With a sharp knife, cut a slice off the root end and top end of an onion. Peel off the brown skin.

Cut the onion in half from top to root.

Lay each half of the onion down on its cut side with the root to your left (or right if you are left-handed).

Slice downwards in slices $\frac{1}{4}$ ins apart from root to tip (without quite touching the root) so the onion is held together.

Now slice horizontally from the top, without cutting through the root.

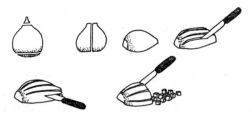

Finally cut downwards across the onion and it will fall into tiny squares.

Repeat with other onion half.

If your cooking should go wrong

Don't be dismayed if the first time you try, some of your efforts are literally a flop. They may well taste very good and that is what matters — and they will have the home-made look!

Next time, follow the recipe very carefully and you are sure to have better luck. Practice never makes perfect in cooking, but it does help.

10

Lunch and Supper

Eggs in the Oven

A baked egg is surprisingly different from a boiled or poached one. You can tuck underneath the egg whatever your imagination or the kitchen comes up with, and make a simple but tasty meal.

For as many people as you have eggs. Or as many eggs as you have people.

Oven time: 5–10 minutes
Oven setting: electric 350° F, gas No. 4

1 egg per person (more if you are hungry)
1 tablespoon cream or top of the milk per egg
Salt, pepper

Bits and pieces for underneath. Choose from:

a small slice of ham	a slice of tomato
a piece of fried bacon	a small piece of fried bread
1 tablespoon grated cheese	some left-over vegetables
a few cooked mushrooms	a few herbs

Turn on the oven.
   Cover the bottom of small ovenproof dishes or the sections of of a bun tin with the filling you choose. Break an egg into a cup and carefully tip it on top. Pour on the cream or top of the milk and season with a little salt and pepper.

Cook for 5–10 minutes, or until the eggs are set, but not rock-hard. If you shake the dishes, the white should stay firm but the yolk still wobble. Then eat up quickly. Remember to wear oven gloves if you handle hot dishes.

Or try the same method with the eggs using a scooped-out baked potato as your 'dish'. Bake the potatoes first for 45 minutes in the oven at 350° F or gas No. 4. Hold the potato with a thick cloth and slice off the top. Scoop out the middle, add your filling, and drop the egg into the hole. Then cook as above.

MINCE MATTERS: Mince meat has an unfair image. 'Monday mince' sounds mean and thin. In fact, mince can be great. It's cheap and quick and adaptable. Mince mixed with an egg and seasonings makes meatballs and hamburgers. Curiously, their different shapes make them taste quite different. Mince cooked with tomatoes makes Greek Shepherd's Pie and Italian Spaghetti Bolognese.

Meat Balls

½ lb (200 gms) minced beef
(or lamb or pork or veal)
1 egg yolk
1 small onion, chopped
(if you like onion)
A pinch of salt and pepper

Few drops Worcestershire
sauce
A tiny pinch of cinnamon
(it is surprisingly nice)
1 tablespoon of flour
1 tablespoon oil or fat

Chop the onion if you are using one.
Mix all the ingredients except the flour and oil or fat in a large bowl. Use your *clean* hands if you like.
Take teaspoonfuls of the mixture and roll it into 8 small balls.

14

Put the flour on a large plate and roll each ball in the flour.

Turn on the stove. Heat the oil or fat in a frying-pan and fry the balls slowly and carefully, turning them once with a fish slice. They should be cooked right through in 10–15 minutes. To cut a dash you can spear each cooked meat ball with a toothpick.

They are also good with tomato sauce. See recipe on p. 18.

Hamburgers

Frying time : 10–15 mins

Meat ball mixture
4 soft rolls

Follow the recipe for meat balls above, but form the mixture into 4 thin rounds. Fry as for meat balls.

Lift out carefully with a fish slice and slide the hamburger into the split roll. You can toast the cut side of the roll first if you want. Serve with a slice of raw onion, mustard, and ketchup.

Greek Shepherd's Pie

This is like the familiar Shepherd's Pie but instead of mashed potato there's an eggy-cheesy-yoghurty topping. Even if you think you don't like yoghurt, try it this way. It's delicious. The recipe is based on a Greek dish called Moussaka. Shepherds love it!

This will serve four timid appetites or two hearty ones.

Oven time : 30 minutes
Oven setting : electric 350° F, gas No. 4

½ lb (200 gms) minced beef
  or lamb
1 onion, chopped
1 tablespoon oil

1 small tin tomatoes
A pinch of salt and pepper
3 tablespoons *plain* yoghurt
1 egg

Turn on oven.
  Part 1: Chop the onion into small pieces. Heat the oil in a frying-pan. Fry the onion until it softens. Add the meat, salt and pepper. Break the meat up with a fork and fry it for a few minutes until it is brown. Open the tin of tomatoes. Add them to the meat mixture and continue cooking quite fast until the liquid has nearly dried up. Empty the mixture into a small oven-proof dish.
  Part 2: Break the egg into a bowl. Add the yoghurt. Beat them together and pour them on top of the meat. Sprinkle with grated cheese.
  Cook in the oven for 30 minutes.

16

Spaghetti Bolognese

Italians reckon that for a long happy life you should eat spaghetti once a day! When you have mastered the art of cooking it to the right texture you might want to do just that.

Sauce:

Follow Part I of the recipe for Greek Shepherd's Pie, but leave the mixture quite runny. Let it simmer very very gently in the pan while you cook the spaghetti.

Spaghetti:

Boil a large saucepanful of water, with a teaspoon of salt and a teaspoon of cooking oil in it. The oil will help to stop the spaghetti sticking together. Add the spaghetti. Read the packet instructions for quantity. What looks like a small amount of spaghetti becomes a lot when cooked, and I find one packet feeds six big appetites. If the spaghetti is the long variety (the best) first break it in half. Cook as long as the packet suggests, probably about 10 minutes, stirring occasionally. To test for doneness, fish out a piece with a long-handled fork, let it cool, and bite it. The spaghetti should be soft but *not* mushy. Beware of cooking spaghetti too long, or it will become a gluey mess. Strain into a sieve which you have put in the sink. Turn it into a bowl and empty the sauce from the frying-pan on top. Sprinkle with grated cheese.

Tomato Sauce

Use this useful sauce for spaghetti (and call it Spaghetti Napoletana), and with meat balls.

1 tablespoon oil
1 tin of tomatoes
A pinch of salt and pepper
1 teaspoon sugar

A pinch of herbs – try basil
A few drops Worcestershire
sauce

Heat the oil in a saucepan. Open the tin of tomatoes and carefully pour in. Add the seasoning and cook gently, stirring with a wooden spoon, for 5 minutes or until the tomatoes have broken up and the sauce seems thickened. It is ready, already.

IT'S BATTER FOR YOU! Batter is a mixture of flour, egg and milk, and as the name suggests it needs to be beaten well to make it good. Don't overbeat though so that the mixture loses its air bubbles. The basic batter recipe can be turned into Pancakes, Yorkshire Pudding, or that often dreadful meal, Toad in the Hole. But using the recipe in this book, your magic touch with a wooden spoon will turn the 'toad' into a princely dish.

Cheese Pancakes

Basic batter:

4 ounces (100 gms) plain
    flour
¼ teaspoon salt
1 egg
A little lard or cooking oil

½ pint (3 dl) milk (or ¼ pint
    [1·5 dl] water and ¼ pint
    [1·5 dl] milk)
4 tablespoons grated cheddar
    cheese

Sift the flour and salt into a basin.

Break the egg into a cup. Make a hollow in the flour with the back of a tablespoon and drop in the egg. Add a little of the milk. Stir the egg and milk with a wooden spoon, gradually drawing in the flour. Add the rest of the milk little by little. When all the milk is stirred into the flour and the mixture is smooth,

beat it with your wooden spoon until little air bubbles appear. Sieve it into a jug. Add the cheese and stir.

In a small frying-pan, heat a teaspoonful of oil. Pour a tablespoon of the mixture from the jug into the centre of the frying pan. Tilt the pan so the mixture runs all over the bottom. Cook for about 2 minutes or until the edges look brown and crispy.

Turn over the pancake with a fish slice and cook the other side.

Take it out of the pan, put it on a plate. Now repeat the performance until you have used up all the batter.

Note: the first pancake is always the worst. Sometimes it's best to throw it away.

You can wrap your pancakes round one of these fillings:

Fillings:

A small tin of baked beans, heated up
Any left-over meat or vegetables, *well* heated up, sizzly hot
A fried egg

Some fried bacon
A small tin of sweetcorn, heated up
Well-fried sausages, or Frankfurter sausages

Yorkshire Pudding

I think the best thing about Sunday lunch is Yorkshire pudding. It's pancake batter cooked in a hot oven. That's all.

Oven time : 40 minutes
Oven setting : electric 400° F, gas No. 5

Turn on the oven.
 Make the batter from the Cheese Pancake recipe, but without the cheese.
 Put 2 tablespoonfuls of oil or lard or dripping in a cake tin or put one teaspoon in each section of a Yorkshire pudding tin or bun tin. Put the tin with the oil into the oven for 15 minutes. Remove it carefully, using oven gloves. Pour the batter into the tin and put it back in the oven. Wait patiently for 25 minutes then check to see if it has become puffed up and golden. Test it by sticking a thin skewer into the middle. If it comes out with batter still sticking to it give it another 5 or 10 minutes.
 Yorkshire pudding makes a delicious dessert with Golden Syrup poured over it.

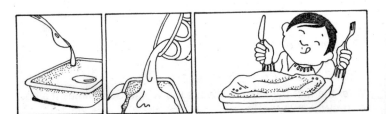

Toad in the Hole

Toad in the Hole is really sausages sitting in Yorkshire pudding. You could use lamb chops instead. Then you could call it Sheep in the Fold!

Oven time: 45 minutes
Oven setting: electric 400° F, gas No. 5

4 fat sausages *or* 8 skinny
  sausages
1 tablespoon fat or oil or
  dripping

Batter from Cheese Pancake
recipe, without the cheese

Turn on the oven. Make your batter. If the sausages are large cut each one into 4 pieces; small ones can be cut in half. Put them with the oil or fat into a small roasting tin or a large cake tin. Put the tin in the oven for 15 minutes. Remove the tin carefully, using oven gloves. Now pour on the batter and replace quickly in the oven. Check after 30 minutes to see if the batter has become a golden crust around the meat. If it still looks a little soggy, award it extra time.

Sweet Pancakes

Make up the batter recipe for Cheese Pancakes, but leave out the cheese. Follow the instructions for frying the pancakes. Serve them sprinkled with sugar and a squeeze of lemon juice over the top.

Or put a spoonful of jam inside and roll them up. Sprinkle with sugar. If you have a baby in the house, pinch a tin of pureed apple, heat it up, and use as a filling! Roll them around a banana, sprinkle with sugar and serve with cream if it is available.

Gratie Taties

The Irish call this delicious potato pancake, *Boxty*. In Jewish cookery it is called *Latkes*. The English have no name for it, so I have made one up.

1 lb (400 gms) potatoes
2 tablespoons flour
1 egg

$\frac{1}{4}$ pint (1·5 dl) milk
Salt and pepper
Cooking oil

Peel the potatoes and grate them on the large holes of the grater into a mixing bowl. Add the flour. Beat the egg with the milk, salt and pepper. Add this liquid mixture to potato and flour. The mixture should be soft enough to drop from a spoon. If it isn't, add a little more milk.

Heat a dessert spoon of oil in a frying-pan. When it is hot pour in a tablespoonful of the potato mixture. After a minute or two when the bottom side is brown, turn it with a fish slice. Cook the other side until brown and crispy. If you have a large frying pan you can cook several taties at once. If not, keep each tatie warm in the oven set to 200° F (electric oven) or gas No. 1.

These are very good with eggs, sausages or bacon.

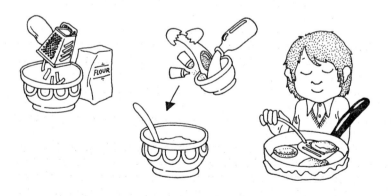

Chocolate Mousse

I've never met anyone in my life who disliked chocolate mousse, which seems a good reason for knowing the recipe.

1 ounce (25 gms) plain
  chocolate per person
1 egg per person

1 tablespoon of water or
  coffee

Break the chocolate into squares. Put it with the water or coffee into the top half of the double boiler.

Set the double boiler on a low heat on the stove and let the chocolate slowly melt.

Separate the eggs (see Useful Advice section). Beat the yolks in a large mixing bowl.

Take the melted chocolate off the stove and let it cool.

Stir the egg yolks into it.

Beat the egg whites in another large bowl with a clean egg beater. Beat them until they are stiff and snowy and hold their shape. (If you get any yolk at all in the egg whites they will not become stiff and snowy or hold their shape however much you beat them.)

Mix the chocolate and egg yolk mixture into the egg whites using a metal spoon. Mix them lightly, lifting the mixture with the spoon, rather than stirring them round and round. This is called *folding in*. Pour the mousse into a dish or individual dishes. Leave it in the refrigerator or cool place to set. It will be ready in a few hours.

Baked Apples

This is a good pudding to make when something else is cooking in the oven. If you have an egg white left over from another recipe you can make Snowy Baked Apples which are spectacular!

Oven time: 45 minutes

Oven setting: electric 350°F, gas No. 4

1 apple for each person
  (cooking or eating apples
  both work)
Butter or margarine
Apricot jam or Redcurrant jelly

1 tablespoon raisins or
  sultanas for each person *or*
  1 tablespoon mixed nuts
  and raisins
Brown sugar

Optional

1 egg white

2 tablespoons castor sugar

If the oven is not already used, turn it on.

With a pointed knife make a slit in the skin of the apple around the middle. This stops the apple skin bursting in the oven. If you have an apple corer use it to take the core out of each apple, or do it carefully with a knife. Place the cored apples in a baking tin.

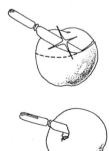

Fill the centre of each apple with raisins, sultanas or a mixture of nuts and raisins. At Christmas time you could use a spoonful of mince meat.

Sprinkle brown sugar on top of each apple and then top with a small piece of butter or margarine. Finally spread a spoonful of jam or jelly on top of each apple.

Add a teacup of water to the baking tin and bake the apples in the oven for 45 minutes or until they are soft and sticky.

Snowy Baked Apples

Half an hour before the apples are done, beat the egg white with an egg beater until it is stiff and snowy and standing up in peaks. Add the sugar and beat again until the mixture is shiny and holds its shape. Using oven gloves remove the baking tin from the oven. Drop a spoonful of the mixture (or meringue as it's now called) onto the top of each apple. With oven gloves replace the tin in the oven for 30 minutes. Each apple will be covered with a glistening fall of snow!

Parties and Drinks

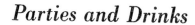

Scones

Some people say scone to rhyme with 'stone'. Some people say scone to rhyme with 'on'. Either way, home-made and eaten warm with jam and butter (or better still whipped cream) they are a must for a really good tea party.

Oven time: 10–12 minutes
Oven setting: electric 450° F, gas No. 8

8 ounces (200 gms) plain
  flour *and*
2 teaspoons baking powder

or
8 ounces (200 gms)
  self-raising flour

plus

1–2 ounces (25–50 gms)
  butter, or margarine, or soft
  margarine

1 teaspoon salt
$\frac{1}{4}$ pint (1·5 dl) milk

Turn on the oven.

Sift the baking powder and flour, or the self-raising flour, into a bowl. Mix in the salt.

Using your fingers, rub the fat into the flour until it becomes a mass of tiny lumps. If you use soft margarine stir it in with a wooden spoon.

Add half the milk and press the mixture together. If it seems too dry and crumbly add a little more milk, until you have a dough that can be rolled; not too dry and not too sticky.

Flour a board or table and your rolling pin and roll the dough out into a piece about $\frac{1}{2}$ inch (12 mm) thick. With a biscuit-cutter or upturned egg cup, cut out the scones. Dip the cutter into a pile of flour between cutting each scone to stop it sticking to the dough. The odd-shaped pieces left can be gathered together and rolled out again. And again.

Rub a baking sheet with a little butter or oil and put the scones on this with a little space between them; they spread as they cook. Any left-over milk can be brushed on top of each scone to give it a golden brown top when it is cooked. Place the baking tray on the middle shelf in the oven and cook for 10–12 minutes. Eat when warm, split in two and buttered and jammed.

Nutty Puffs

Puff pastry is complicated to make and the frozen variety is very good. Buy a packet a few hours or a day in advance as you must let it thaw before it can be rolled. You could use any left-over pastry for sausage rolls (the recipe is in the Picnics section).

Oven time: 15 minutes
Oven setting: electric 425° F,
   gas No. 7

One packet frozen puff pastry
3 tablespoons condensed milk
2 ounces (50 gms) chopped walnuts
2 ounces (50 gms) raisins or sultanas
2 ounce (50 gms) bar of plain
   chocolate

Turn on the oven.
   Roll the thawed-out pastry on a floured board until it is as thin as a 10p piece. Cut it into squares about 3" (76 mm) in size.
   Grate the chocolate into a bowl.
   Add the nuts, raisins and milk and mix together.
   Put a teaspoonful of the mixture in the centre of each square of pastry.
   Fold one half of the pastry over to make a triangle and press the edges firmly together.
   Brush with any left-over condensed milk and sprinkle with a little sugar.
   Grease a baking tray with butter or oil and place the puffs on it in rows. Bake for 15 minutes on the middle shelf until they are puffed up and golden brown.

Sponge Cake

This cake has three virtues. It is quick, easy, and not expensive. On the other hand it doesn't keep very well, but I don't suppose it will get the chance!

Oven time: 15–20 minutes
Oven setting: electric 375° F, gas No. 5

4 ounces (100 gms) of soft margarine	4 ounces (100 gms) castor sugar
4 ounces (100 gms) self-raising flour	1 level teaspoon baking powder
2 eggs	

Turn on the oven.

Put a small piece of butter or margarine on a piece of paper and grease two small sponge tins. Put a dessertspoonful of flour in each tin and shake it around to cover the tin in flour. Shake out any loose flour. Put all the ingredients into a large bowl and beat with a wooden spoon until they are well mixed and light. Divide the mixture between the two tins and flatten the top with a knife. Bake in the oven for 15–20 minutes. To test if the cake is done, press *lightly* with your finger in the middle of the sponge; the dent you make should spring back.

Remove the tins from the oven. Let them cool. Run a knife around the edge of the cakes and turn them on to a wire rack. To get them the right way up, put a plate on top of the cake and turn the whole thing over.

The two cakes can be sandwiched together with jam.

To make a simple decoration on top, either find a paper doily or cut out a pattern in paper as a stencil. Lay this on the top of the top layer of the cake and sprinkle icing sugar evenly all over. Shaking it through a sieve is the best way. Carefully remove the paper and you will have a sugar stencil. Or ice it.

Water Icing

8 ounces (200 gms) icing sugar	1 tablespoon orange juice or lemon juice
1 tablespoon water	Colouring (if you like)

Sieve the icing sugar into a basin. Heat the water, mix it with the juice and add a little at a time to the icing sugar, beating well until the icing coats the spoon and is shiny.

If you want to colour it, dip a skewer into the bottle of colour and add a drop at a time while you stir until you get the shade you want. Remember bright red icing is *most* unappetising.

Pour the icing onto the cakes and spread with a knife dipped into hot water. Keep dipping it while you work.

Decorate with chocolate drops, sugared strands, jelly babies, silver balls or whatever you have to hand.

You can bake this same cake mixture in paper cake cases or a bun tin to make fairy cakes. These are good with icing too.

Fancy Sandwiches

One day the Earl of Sandwich was busy gambling. He was enjoying himself so much that he couldn't be bothered to stop for a meal. So he slapped a piece of beef between two slices of bread – and started a whole new way of eating. When *you* are busy playing you probably only want a simple sandwich – ham or cheese – but these recipes are for when you're entertaining friends.

Here are some fillings:

Tuna fish
Open a small tin of tuna fish (drain off the oil) and empty the fish into a bowl. Add a tablespoon of mayonnaise or salad cream, some salt and pepper. For crunchiness add a stick of celery chopped into small pieces, or a raw chopped onion. Mix well.

Saucy Egg
Hard boil two eggs by boiling them for 10 minutes and then run cold water over them in the saucepan until they are cool. Peel them, chop them and mix with 1 tablespoon tomato sauce, 1 teaspoon Worcestershire Sauce, salt and pepper. If you have some parsley, chop a few sprigs and mix it in.

Cheese and Apple
Core the apple and slice it downwards into thin slices. Grate some cheddar cheese. Put a layer of cheese, a layer of apple slices, into the sandwich.

Sardine and Tomato
Open a small tin of sardines and pour off the oil. Empty the sardines into a bowl. Chop up one large or two small tomatoes.

32

Add a little soft butter or margarine and mash everything together with a fork. Season with a pinch of salt and pepper.

Triple Decker Sandwiches, made with brown and white bread and two fillings, look attractive.

Open Sandwiches look pretty. Use just the bottom slice of bread and decorate your choice of filling with slices of cucumber, egg, tomato. Sprigs of parsley lend a professional air.

Rolled Sandwiches must be made with very new bread. Trim the crusts from a slice. Butter it and lay on a piece of thinly sliced ham or any soft filling. Roll the sandwich up and cut into rounds. They will look like pinwheels.

Fried Sandwich
Butter two slices of bread. Spread the unbuttered side of one piece of bread with tomato ketchup. Place on top one slice of cheese then the other slice of bread, with buttered side outside.

Fry the sandwich in a little extra butter, first on one side and then on the other. Cut into quarters.

Cinnamon Toast
Toast lightly as many slices of bread as you want. For each slice, mix together a heaped teaspoon of sugar with a pinch of cinnamon. Butter the toast while it is still warm and spread with the mixture of sugar and cinnamon. Pop the bread under the grill for a minute so that the sugar melts a little.

Orange Jelly Fruit

Sliced carefully, after making, these orange jellies look like slices of real orange but with jelly where there should be fruit.

Packet of jelly. Orange jelly   3 oranges
   looks most natural, but you
   can use any flavour you like

Cut the oranges in half and squeeze out the juice into a measuring jug, without breaking the orange skins.

As carefully as you can scrape out the white skin and pith from the inside of the orange halves. A small teaspoon is best for this.

Make up the jelly using the strained orange juice as part of the liquid. Make it up according to the instructions on the packet *but with a teacupful less water than the packet advises.* This makes the jelly firm enough to cut.

Pour the dissolved jelly into the orange halves.
Leave the oranges to set in the refrigerator or a cool place.
When it is really firm, slice the orange halves in two.

ICE-CREAM is surprisingly easy to make, and once you have
mastered the basic method you can dream up any flavour you
please. The two basic ingredients are a refrigerator and the
patience to wait for the mixture to freeze!

Vanilla Ice-cream

1 pint (6 dl) milk   2 egg yolks
3 ounces (75 gms) of sugar $\frac{1}{4}$ pint (1·5 dl) whipping cream
A piece of vanilla pod *or*   or double cream
   vanilla essence

Separate the eggs (see Useful Advice section). Beat the egg
yolks. Store the egg whites in a covered cup in the refrigerator.
Put the milk, egg yolks and vanilla pod (or three drops of vanilla

essence) into the top saucepan of a double boiler or a mixing bowl which will fit into a saucepan without touching its base. Fill the bottom saucepan with hot water to just below the level of the top pan or bowl. Put the whole contraption on the stove on a low heat. Cook the mixture gently, stirring all the time until it thickens. Do not let the water in the bottom saucepan boil or the mixture might curdle. When the custard (which is what you have made) coats the back of the spoon, it is ready.

Let the custard cool, and remove the vanilla pod if you have used one. Whip the cream until it is thick but not stiff and mix it into the cooled custard. Put the mixture into an ice tray and cover with foil. Place it in the freezing compartment of the refrigerator.

One hour later remove the tray and stir the ice-cream. This is to stop icy lumps forming. Return the tray to the freezing compartment and leave for another hour at least.

Everything on a Sundae

A popular idea at parties is to let your guests make up their own
ice-cream sundaes. Lay out different flavours of ice-cream, a
bowl of chopped nuts, some chopped cherries, slices of banana
and one or two sauces. Each guest can put together a sumptuous
sundae.

Chocolate Sauce

2 ounces (50 gms) plain
   chocolate
2 ounces (50 gms) sugar

2 level teaspoons cornflour
½ pint (3 dl) water

Grate the chocolate into a saucepan.
   Add sugar and cornflour and mix until smooth with a little of
the water. Add the rest of the water and bring to the boil.
Simmer for 5 minutes stirring occasionally.

Toffee Sauce

3 ounces (75 gms) brown sugar   1 ounce (25 gms) butter
2 tablespoons Golden Syrup   4 tablespoons cream

Put all the ingredients into a saucepan. Heat them slowly until they melt and combine. *Do not boil.* Give a good stir.

Golden Sauce

Heat 3 tablespoons Golden Syrup until hot but not boiling.

DRINKS: Did you know that a product labelled 'lemon' or 'orange' drink need not have even a whiff of the fruit in it? So to be clever and healthy, make your own!

Lemonade

4 lemons   2 pints (1·2 litres) boiling
4 ounces (100 gms) sugar   water

Peel the lemons with a potato peeler to get off just the yellow part of the rind. Put the rind in a jug with the sugar. Measure two pints of water (use a milk bottle if necessary) and pour it into the kettle. Boil the water and pour it onto the rinds and sugar. Stir until the sugar dissolves. Leave until cold. Squeeze the lemons and pour in the juice through a strainer. Serve with ice.

Ice-cream Sodas

Orange juice and lemon juice are very nice, but I must say it, Ice-cream Sodas are better.

The easiest way to make them is to put a scoop of ice-cream in the bottom of a tall glass and pour on Coca-Cola or lemonade. To go the whole hog, spoon on a tablespoon of whipped cream.

Guy Fawkes,
Barbecues,
Camp Fire Cookery

be very
careful

These are ideas for food you can actually cook on or in a fire and recipes for dishes you prepare inside that warm your insides, outside.

Toffee Apples

(*N.B. Sugar boils at a very high temperature and can burn you badly. Always take special care when you are making sweets and have an adult on hand.*)

Ask an adult to be around for these.

6 small hard dessert apples
½ lb (200 gms) granulated or
    lump sugar
½ pint (3 dl) water

Wooden skewers or ice-lolly
    sticks
1 Adult

Wash and dry the apples. Oil a sheet of foil or a baking tray. Push the sticks firmly into the apples at the stalk end. In a thick-bottomed pan mix the sugar and water and put it on a low heat on the stove. Heat slowly until the sugar melts and then turn the heat up a little and boil until the mixture begins to turn brown. Don't stir as this makes bubbles. If it is browning unevenly *ask an adult* to tilt the pan and swirl the mixture round. When it is golden brown, take it off the heat and wearing oven gloves pick up each

apple and twirl it in the toffee. When it is evenly coated, set it on the oiled foil. Work quickly so that the toffee does not have time to set in the pan. Place the apples apart from each other, otherwise you will have inseparable twins. Toffee apples do not keep longer than a day.

Barbecued Baked Beans

This is a spicy version of the old old favourite.

1 tablespoon vegetable oil
1 onion
1 tablespoon tomato ketchup
1 tablespoon treacle
1 teaspoon mustard
1 teaspoonful water

1 teaspoon Worcestershire
sauce
1 very large tin baked beans
2 Frankfurter sausages
(if you want)

Heat the oil in a saucepan. Slice the onion as finely as possible. Fry the onion until it is soft. Add the ketchup, treacle, mustard, Worcestershire sauce and water. Stir and cook for a few minutes. (If you want to use the Frankfurters, cut them into inch-long [25 mm] pieces and add them now.) Open the tin of beans and

add to the saucepan. Stir carefully to blend in the sauce and heat very slowly until everything is piping hot.

If you have time, a hollowed-out loaf (see Picnics section), buttered and warmed through in the oven, makes a very good 'pot' for these beans. Place the loaf on a serving dish before you fill it.

CAMP FIRE FOOD: These recipes are for cooking on a barbecue or on a grill over a camp fire. To improvise a grill you can use a shelf from the oven (if your mother doesn't mind).

Kebabs

You can buy special Kebab Skewers but ordinary meat skewers which your butcher might sell you, will do just as well.

For 4 skewers:

4 large sausages	1 onion
2 tomatoes	Cooking oil
4 pieces of bacon	*1 Adult*
8 mushrooms (optional)	

Cut each sausage into 4. Cut each tomato into quarters.
Cut each bacon piece in half and roll up neatly.
Peel the onion and cut into quarters.

On each skewer thread a piece of sausage, a piece of bacon, a piece of tomato, a piece of onion, and then repeat. Brush the loaded skewers with oil. Grill them on the barbecue, turning them wearing oven gloves. As they cook brush them with a little more oil. Make sure the sausage is cooked all the way through before eating.

Hawaiian Kebabs: Wrap each piece of bacon round a cube of tinned pineapple.

43

Chicken Parcels

4 small pieces of chicken
(drumsticks and wings are
good)
2 tablespoons cooking oil
1 tablespoon honey
1 tablespoon soya sauce

A pinch of herbs (if you have
them)
Pinch of salt and pepper
A sheet of aluminium foil
1 Adult

Cut the foil into 10-inch (254-mm) squares.

Mix all the ingredients for the sauce in a mixing bowl. If the honey is the stiff kind warm it first in a small saucepan.

Put each chicken piece in the centre of a piece of foil. Turn up the edges to make a basket shape.

Mix the sauce and divide it between the chicken pieces. Join two opposite edges of foil and fold over and over. Tuck the outside edges in and fold the foil right down as far as it will go. You now have a watertight parcel.

44

Bake these parcels on the barbecue turning often for about 20 minutes. Unwrap them wearing oven gloves and if you like, finish the chicken off on the grill to give it a crisp outside. You can brush the remaining sauce over it as it is crisping.

Spare Ribs of Lamb or Pork

1 rack of ribs of lamb or pork	1 tablespoon vinegar
2 tablespoonsful cooking oil	Salt and pepper
2 tablespoons Golden Syrup	*1 Adult*

Mix the oil, syrup and vinegar in a basin.

Salt and pepper the ribs and roast them on the barbecue for 10 minutes. With a pastry brush and wearing oven gloves brush the meat with the syrup and vinegar mixture. Keep brushing and turning the ribs until they are done. These can be done in the oven as well. Roast the ribs first at 350° F electricity, No. 4 gas for 20 minutes and then turn down the heat to 300° F electricity, No. 2 gas for 30 minutes for the cooking and basting.

Cooking actually in the fire is best done when the fire has died down and there are hot smouldering embers. Potatoes cooked in their jackets this way are the best potatoes in the world. Don't attempt to cook in the fire without an adult around.

Baked Potatoes

Scrub some large potatoes. Rub them with a little cooking oil. If the fire is not a big one cook them in the oven first for 30 minutes

at 350° F electricity or No. 4 gas. Ask an adult to bury the potatoes in the hot ashes of the fire. They will take 30 minutes if pre-cooked or an hour if not. Take them out of the fire with a garden spade. Test for readiness with a skewer. Hold them in gloved hands. Split them open and add salt and butter. And perhaps a slice of cheese, or a scoop of cream cheese.

Roasted Chestnuts

Rub the chestnuts with a little oil and pierce the skin with a skewer (this stops them exploding). Heap them on a garden spade and rest its metal part on the embers of the fire. Ask an adult to heap hot ashes on top. Chestnuts will take about 45 minutes. Hold them in gloved hands to eat.

Toasted Marshmallows

Stick a marshmallow on the end of a long stick. Hold it near the flames or embers until the marshmallow begins to bubble and melt. Then lap it up.

Baked Bananas

Bananas can be baked in their skins in the embers of the fire. When the skins have turned black and the bananas are very soft they are ready. Ten minutes is usually long enough. Carefully peel off a strip of skin and eat the lovely gooey flesh out of the banana boat.

Christmas

Things you cook at Christmas make great decorations. And instead of putting them away for next year, you eat them up!

Christmas Tree Biscuits

Sugar Plums

Frosted Fruit

Christmas Tree Biscuits

Oven time : 20 minutes
Oven setting : electric 375° F, gas No. 5

8 ounces (200 gms) flour
4 ounces (100 gms) margarine
4 ounces (100 gms) soft
  brown sugar

1 pinch ground ginger
2 ounces (50 gms) treacle
2 ounces (50 gms) Golden
  Syrup

Turn on the oven.

Sift the flour into a large bowl. Add all the other ingredients. With your hands work the mixture until you have an evenly coloured dough. Flour a board or table-top and your rolling pin. Roll out the dough to about $\frac{1}{8}$ in (3 mm) thickness and it is ready to shape.

If you have gingerbread cutters or animal cutters you can use those. Otherwise, make your own cardboard stencils and cut round them with a knife. *Or* why not cut out letters ? The initials of all the members of your family might be popular.

Decorate your biscuits with currants, silver balls, pieces of chopped glace cherry.

Place the biscuits on a greased baking sheet and bake, on the middle shelf, for 20 minutes or until lightly browned. Cool on a wire rack. The biscuits will stiffen. Using half the icing recipe on p. 31 you can outline the biscuits using an icing cone (see illustration).

Sugar Plums

Who would have thought prunes could be so good ?

$\frac{1}{2}$ lb (200 gms) large
  Californian tenderized
  prunes (stoneless)

8 ounces (200 gms) sugar
extra sugar (castor)
1 Adult

Put the prunes in a bowl and cover with boiling water. Allow to stand for 5 minutes.

Drain them in a sieve. Put them back in the bowl. Cover them again with boiling water. Let stand 5 minutes and drain.

Put the prunes and sugar in a saucepan. Just cover them with cold water. Bring slowly to the boil and simmer gently until the prunes are plump and tender and the syrup has thickened. It will take about 10 minutes. On a plate sprinkle a handful of castor sugar. Spear a prune with a fork, let the hot syrup drip back into the saucepan and roll the prune in the sugar. Repeat.

Leave for 8 hours in a warm place to dry. Store in a jar.

Frosted Fruit

A pile of frosted fruit makes a beautiful table decoration. Frost a few nuts too, to fill in the corners. There are two methods.

With an egg white:

Choose the fruit to be frosted. Grapes are easy to do and look very pretty. Tangerine segments must be carefully pulled apart so the skin is intact, otherwise the juice will melt the frosting. Whole apples and pears are spectacular. Try nuts: use shelled almonds, walnuts or brazils.

Separate the egg (see Useful Advice section). Put the yolk in a covered cup in the refrigerator or a cool place. Put the white in a mixing bowl and beat with a fork. Beat it until it is bubbly but not stiff. Have ready a plate sprinkled thickly with castor sugar. Take a grape (or other fruit) by the stem twirl it in the egg white and then in the sugar. Lay it on a foil-covered plate or a sheet of greaseproof paper. Let the fruit harden in a cool place. Eat the same day.

With a syrup:

4 ounces (100 gms) sugar	more sugar
½ pint (3 dl) water	*1 Adult*

Have your fruit ready, it must be dry. Grease a baking sheet. Put the sugar and water in a saucepan. Bring slowly to the boil while the sugar melts. When the sugar has melted boil the mixture quite fast. After five minutes dip a wooden spoon in and let the drips fall into a cup of cold water. If they harden immediately, the syrup is ready. If not, boil a little longer and try again. Remove from the heat. Wearing oven gloves quickly twirl the fruit in the syrup, holding it by the stems or with a fork. Nuts can be dropped in and fished out quickly with a fork. Let the fruit and nuts harden on the greased tray in a cool place. Eat the same day.

Stringing Popcorn

1 packet of popcorn   LARGE saucepan with a lid
1 tablespoon oil

Buy a packet of popcorn and pop it according to the instructions on the packet. If there are no instructions the standard method is to heat the oil in the saucepan. Empty in your corn. Don't put in too much at once. Put the saucepan lid on firmly and wait for a popping noise. When tiny little guns seem to be going off, shake the pan so the popcorn does not stick or burn. When the popping stops, remove from the heat.

When it is cool, string the popcorn like a necklace with a needle and long thread. It makes a lovely Christmas decoration.

Popcorn Balls

Place your popped corn in a large mixing bowl.

Make the syrup in the Frosted Fruit recipe.

When it is ready, pour it over the corn and stir with a long wooden spoon. With two tablespoons form the popcorn into balls. When it is cooler you can press it together with your hands, having first rubbed your hands with a little oil. You can hang these balls from the tree but they will not last as well as the strings of popcorn.

Christmas Log

This is cheating, not cooking, but it's fun to do.

1 large chocolate swiss roll (un-iced)

For the icing

4 ounces (100 gms) soft
  margarine or butter
6 ounces (150 gms) sieved
  icing sugar

2 ounces (50 gms) melted
  plain chocolate

Place two pieces of greaseproof paper, over-lapping, on a meat dish.

Put the swiss roll on top, with the join of the paper midway beneath.

In a bowl beat the icing sugar into the margarine or butter. Beat well with a wooden spoon until it is light and creamy. Melt the chocolate on a plate over a saucepan of hot water. Scrape it off into the bowl and beat well until it is all mixed in.

Cut a thin slice off the roll. Cut it in half. Match one half on top of the other. Trim the curved end off and eat. Lay the 'twig' shape beside the cake. Now ice the log and the 'twig' all over. Rough up the surface of the icing with a fork to resemble bark. Sprinkle with a little icing sugar for a snowy effect. If you have some holly place a sprig on top. Pull the paper out from under the log.

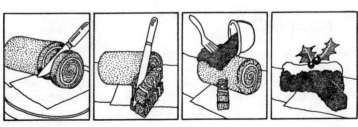

Breakfast

Sunday makes a good 'Be Good to Your Parents Day' – a day when you give them breakfast in bed. You'll have to get up early to get it ready.

Laying the Tray

Arrange a few flowers, if there are any around, in an egg cup or small vase.

Fold a napkin cleverly, a paper one will do.

Take up the papers. Or write a letter. Or do a drawing.

Making the Breakfast

If there are several oranges in the house, squeeze one or two to make a glass of fresh orange juice.

Or using a pointed knife cut round half a grapefruit, take out the segments with a spoon and put in a glass. Sprinkle with a little sugar.

Choose one of the following recipes as the main part of breakfast.

Bacon and Egg Open Sandwich

Oven setting: electric 200° F, gas No. 1

Turn on the oven.

Fry two rashers of bacon and keep them warm on a plate in the oven.

Fry one thin slice of bread in the bacon fat. You may need to add a little more butter or oil. Put the bread with the bacon in the oven.

Fry an egg gently in the remaining fat.

Using oven gloves, remove the bread and bacon from the oven. Put the bacon on the bread, then the egg on the bacon. Take it in quickly before it has time to get cold.

American Egg

Toast one slice of bread, and butter it.

Fill a saucepan with cold water.

Take an egg. If it is straight from the refrigerator run it under warm water from the tap. This is to prevent it breaking in the pan. Lower it gently into the water in the pan. Set the pan on the stove and bring the water to the boil. Time the egg from the moment the water boils. Give it 3–4 minutes depending on the size of the egg (a big egg will take 4 minutes).

Remove the egg from the pot with a spoon. Holding it in a cloth, tap it all over very gently with a knife, until it is cracked all over. Now peel it carefully. Place the peeled egg in a cup. Cut the toast into fingers. Take the egg, toast, salt and pepper on the tray, and don't forget a teaspoon. The toast is dipped into the runny yolk, and there are no pieces of shell to get in between the sheets!

Tomatoes on Toast

Slice two tomatoes in half. Sprinkle the cut sides with a little salt and pepper and put a pat of butter on each. Grill them slowly until they are soft right through.

While they are cooking make a slice of toast, and butter it while it is still warm.

Lay the cooked tomatoes neatly on top.

Making a Good Pot of Tea

Boil a kettle of fresh water. Water that has already been boiled goes 'flat'.

If you have very hot water in the tap you can warm the teapot by rinsing it out. Experts say it makes no difference to the final cup of tea.

Put in a teaspoonful of tea for each person.

When the water has just come to the boil, turn off the heat and carefully pour the water onto the tea. Let it 'make' for 3 or 4 minutes. Now it is ready.

Indoors on a
Rainy Afternoon

MAKING SWEETS: Sweets like toffee and fudge involve boiling a syrup to a high temperature. Sugar boils at a much higher temperature than water. So when you are making these sweets you *must* have an adult around to help you. It is also a great help to have a jam or sweet thermometer to tell you when the mixture has reached the right temperature. The other method of testing the temperature is to drop a little of the mixture into a bowl of cold water. The different recipes will tell you what to look for.

Toffee

4 ounces (100 gms) demerara
  sugar
4 ounces (100 gms) butter or
  margarine

2 tablespoons Golden Syrup
1 small tin of condensed milk
1 Adult

Oil a shallow (preferably square) cake tin.

Put all the ingredients into a large saucepan and bring them slowly to the boil stirring all the while with a wooden spoon. Boil for 5 minutes then begin to test the toffee. Dip your wooden spoon into the mixture and let some of the toffee drip into a bowl of cold water. When it sets hard at once, the toffee is ready. If you are using a thermometer it should register 268°F.

Take the pan off the heat at once and pour the mixture into the oiled tin. When it starts to set mark it in squares with a knife. Leave it to cool and set completely, then break the toffee into squares. If you don't eat it all at once, you can store it in an airtight tin.

Raisin or Nut Toffee
Mix in two tablespoons of raisins or chopped nuts just before you pour the mixture into the tin.

Fudge

1 lb (400 gms) soft brown
  sugar
2 ounces (50 gms) butter
  or margarine

$\frac{1}{2}$ pint (3 dl) milk
Vanilla essence
1 Adult

Oil a tin. The shape is not important but a rectangular one is best, about 8 ins × 5 ins (203 mm × 126 mm). Put the sugar, butter and milk into a large saucepan and heat slowly until the sugar has dissolved.

Turn the heat up and bring the mixture to the boil. Boil for 15 minutes. Using a spoon drip some of the mixture into a bowl of cold water. When rubbed between your fingers it should form a soft ball. Keep boiling and testing until you reach this stage (235° F on a thermometer). Dip a skewer into a bottle of vanilla essence and add a few drops. Take the saucepan off the stove and beat with a wooden spoon until the mixture becomes thick and fudgey. Pour it into your prepared tin and leave to set. Cut it into squares, and enjoy yourself!

SAFE SWEETS

Rocky Road

8 ounces (200 gms) milk chocolate
4 ounces (25 gms) marshmallow

1–4 oz. (25 gms) packet walnut pieces
1 dessertspoon cooking oil

Butter a small cake tin (preferably square).

In a double boiler (or bowl that will fit into a saucepan without touching the bottom) put the chocolate broken into squares. Add the oil. Fill the bottom saucepan with hot water but not touching the bottom of the bowl. Put the whole contraption on the stove. Heat gently until the chocolate melts. Stir to blend. Cut up the marshmallows into small pieces. Spread half the melted chocolate in the cake tin. Dot the marshmallows and nuts all over. Cover with the rest of the chocolate. Cool for at least 8 hours (I'm afraid) and cut into squares with a knife.

Peppermint Creams

8 ounces (200 gms) icing sugar	Peppermint essence 1 egg white

Separate one egg (see Useful Advice section) and put the egg white into a large bowl. Donate the yolk to your Mum.

Sift the icing sugar into a bowl.

Whip the egg white with a fork until it is light and frothy and gradually beat in the icing sugar. When the mixture is stiff you can work in the remaining icing sugar with your hands.

Sugar a board or a table-top and put the mixture on it. Pour $\frac{1}{2}$ teaspoon peppermint essence on top and work it in with your hands. Knead the mixture like dough. When it seems firm and dry roll it out with a rolling pin and cut it into small rounds with the smallest biscuit cutter or an up-turned eggcup. Leave the creams in a cool place to dry. A little melted chocolate poured over adds a classy touch.

Chocolate Crunchies

8 ounces (200 gms) plain chocolate	2 ounces (50 gms) of cornflakes or rice crispies

Grease a baking tin with butter or margarine.

Use a double boiler or find a mixing bowl that fits into a sauce-pan and fill the bottom of the saucepan with hot water to just below the level of the mixing bowl. Break the chocolate into pieces and place in the mixing bowl or top of the double boiler.

Put the whole thing on a low heat on the stove and melt the chocolate. Stir in the cornflakes or rice crispies. With a tablespoon put little mounds of the mixture on to the baking tray and leave to set.

Brownies

Oven time: 30 minutes
Oven setting: electric 325° F, gas No. 3

2 ounces (50 gms) butter or margarine
2 ounces (50 gms) plain chocolate
4 ounces (100 gms) castor sugar
1 egg

2 ounces (50 gms) flour
$\frac{1}{4}$ teaspoon baking powder
Pinch of salt
2 ounces (50 gms) chopped walnuts (optional)
Vanilla essence

Turn on the oven.

Grease a small cake tin, with a little butter or margarine.

Over a very low heat melt the butter and chocolate in a large saucepan.

Remove from the stove, stir well with a wooden spoon, then stir in the sugar. Add the egg and a few drops of vanilla essence off a skewer. Beat well. Quickly stir in the flour, salt and nuts (if you are using them). Spread the mixture in your cake tin. Cook for 30 minutes. Remove the pan using oven gloves, and leave the mixture to cool. It will sink but this is quite right. Before it is quite cold cut it into squares with an oiled knife. The finished cake will have a crisp top and a gooey underneath. This is the special asset of Brownies and is due to using twice as much sugar as flour.

Picnics, or Food to Run Away With

When you're on a picnic someone (not you of course) is bound to say 'Doesn't everything taste better for being eaten outside'. True enough. But it doesn't mean you have to settle down to a fish-paste sandwich and hope the pieces of grass clinging to it will make all the difference. Try some of these ideas when you are setting off on your next expedition.

Saucer Pies

You bake these pies in old china saucers. Remove the pies once they are cooked and you will have an individual meal. For the strong-armed and cautious you can leave them in the saucers for the journey.

Oven time: 30 minutes
Oven setting: 350° F, gas No. 4

Pastry (to make 2 covered pies)

2 ounces (50 gms) soft margarine	4 ounces (100 gms) of plain flour
Water	A pinch of salt

Filling

4 pieces of fried bacon *or*	2 tablespoons milk
2 slices of ham	Pinch of pepper
2 eggs	

Pastry: Grease with margarine two old china saucers.

In a bowl put two tablespoons of flour, the margarine and 1 tablespoon water. Mix together with a fork. Add the rest of the flour and the salt and work into a firm dough.

Flour a board or table-top. Divide the mixture into two. Roll out the first half until about the thickness of a 10p piece. Cut two rounds slightly bigger than your saucers. Line the saucers with the pastry. Prick the pastry with a fork. Roll the second lump of dough in the same way.

Filling: Fry the bacon if that is what you are using. Cut it into small pieces. *Or* cut up the two slices of ham. Beat the ham or bacon with the other filling ingredients in a bowl. Divide the mixture between the two saucers. Dip your finger in a cup of water and dampen the edges of the pastry in the saucers. Cover the saucers with the two remaining pastry rounds and press all round the edges to seal. Brush the tops with a little milk. Place the saucers on a baking sheet and bake for 30 minutes.

Remove and let cool. You can, of course, eat them hot, too.

Submarines

These are real survival rations. Should keep you going for a day. The ideal submarine uses a French loaf but you can hollow out crispy rolls or a whole square loaf.

Cut a French loaf lengthwise through the middle. Or cut a lid off a roll or square loaf.

With a spoon hollow out the two halves of the French loaf or the inside of the roll or loaf, leaving a good covering of bread inside. (The breadcrumbs can be dried in a warm oven, crushed, and kept for coating fish and chicken.)

Line the bread with lettuce leaves. Then arrange a combination of these fillings on top.

Sliced tomatoes	Salami
Sliced cucumber	Sliced hard-boiled egg
Sliced cheese	Sliced onion
Sliced ham	Sardines
Cooked sausage	Radishes
Cooked Frankfurter sausage	Sliced carrots

or whatever else the store-cupboard or your imagination provides.

Season with salt and pepper. A little olive oil is good, if you like it. Spread the bread lid with butter or mayonnaise or salad cream and replace. If you want to slice your submarine it is a good idea to wrap it in foil or greaseproof paper and leave it under weights for a few hours. Tins from the larder balanced on a bread board are ideal.

Hard-boiled Eggs

A picnic wouldn't be a picnic without hard-boiled eggs.

But hard-boiled eggs wouldn't be hard-boiled eggs without salt. So take some salt along screwed up in a piece of paper.

To hard-boil eggs. Place your eggs in a saucepan of cold water. Bring the water to the boil and boil gently for 10 minutes. Take the pan off the heat and put it under the cold tap. Run the water on the eggs until the pan is full of cold water. Leave the eggs in the water until you need them. This will stop a black ring forming round the yolks.

'1000-year-old' Eggs

These look very pretty. Boil the eggs as above. When they are cool enough to handle tap them all over very gently on a hard surface so that the shell is cracked all over. Boil 2 teabags in a fresh saucepan of water and add your cracked eggs. Boil for 10 minutes. When you peel the eggs on the picnic they will have a lovely marble design on them.

Stuffed Eggs

Boil as many eggs as you want following the recipe for hard-boiled eggs. When they are cold cut them carefully in half lengthwise.

Scoop out the yolks into a bowl. Mash the yolk with a fork. Stir in enough mayonnaise to make a firm paste. Add a pinch of salt and pepper. If you like a strong flavour, add a pinch of curry powder. With a teaspoon smooth the yolk mixture back into the white parts of the egg and sandwich the eggs back together again. The filling should hold them together.

Sausage Rolls

Oven time: 20 minutes
Oven setting: electricity 450° F, gas No. 8

½ packet frozen puff pastry
  (use the other half for
  Nutty Puffs)

½ lb (200 gms) chipolata
  sausages
or
Sausage meat

Turn on the oven.
  Make sure the pastry has thawed enough to enable you to roll it.
  Flour a board or table-top and your rolling pin.
  Roll out the pastry into an oblong shape and as thin as a 10p piece.

Divide it in two lengthwise so you have two long pieces of pastry about 4 ins (100 mm) wide.

Shape the sausage meat into sausage-shaped lengths of about 1½ ins (40 mm). Or cut the chipolatas into the same length. Place the sausages at intervals down one side of the pastry leaving gaps of ½ in (12 mm). Fold the pastry over and press down the edges. Cut with a knife between each mound of sausage and press the edges together. Make two diagonal slits on top of each roll. Brush the tops with milk. Put the rolls on to a baking sheet and bake for 20 minutes or until the pastry has risen and is golden brown.

Chocolate Sandwich

This is a French idea. And like a lot of French ideas about food, it is a very good one.

You should have a French loaf, but any fresh white crusty bread will do. Take with you a bar of plain chocolate and the loaf. When it comes to the time for a little sweet something, take two slices of bread and tuck the chocolate in between. Or you can sandwich your chocolate between two 'Marie' biscuits or any plain biscuits. It provides an ideal unsticky end to an outdoor meal.

DRINKS: Cool any bottled drinks in the refrigerator before you leave and then pour them into a thermos for the journey.

Iced Tea

Taking hot tea is a performance as to make it taste right you have to take milk and sugar separately. Try iced tea, which is wonderfully refreshing.

69

Make up a teapotful of strong tea. Strain it into a jug. Squeeze in the juice from half a lemon. Add enough water to make it the strength you like. Add a tablespoon of sugar and taste for sweetness. Add more if you like it sweeter. Leave it to cool, in the refrigerator, if you have one.

The Staff of Life

Making a loaf of bread is one of the most satisfying things you can do. You turn a heap of unappetising flour into a staple food — enough to keep you going for at least a day! A sort of bread can be made simply with flour and water, but bread as we know it always uses a raising agent. Two raising agents are yeast and bicarbonate of soda.

YEAST BREAD: Yeast is actually a living plant and you can help it to thrive by feeding it and keeping it warm, or you can kill it with a very high temperature. Yeast acts as thousands of tiny muscles in the flour, lifting it and making the dough rise. When you put the dough in the oven the yeast stops working and lets the oven get on with cooking. In a cold atmosphere yeast goes to sleep. So we store it in the cold, let it work in the warm and and finish it off in the heat. Dried yeast can be bought in packets and tins. It works well and stores well. You can sometimes buy fresh yeast by the ounce from health-food shops and bakers who bake their own bread. Store it in a cool place in a glass jar with a lid.

A Simple Brown Loaf

There's something specially home-made and wholesome about a brown loaf. Brown (wholemeal) flour can be bought in large supermarkets and stores and in health-food shops.

1 lb (400 gms) brown flour   1 heaped teaspoon salt
1 dessertspoon brown sugar $\frac{1}{2}$ ounce (12 gms) fresh or
   or treacle   dried yeast

Sift the flour and salt into a large mixing bowl.

Pour a little warm water (at body temperature – if you dip your finger in you shouldn't feel it either hot or cold) into a small bowl. Dissolve the sugar or treacle in it. Crumble or sprinkle the yeast on top and leave the bowl in a warm place (by the side of the stove) for the yeast to dissolve and 'feed' on the sugar. After 10 minutes you should see the yeast frothing and bubbles slowly rising. Whisk the mixture with a fork. Pour it into the flour and add enough of the rest of the warm water (also body temperature) to enable you to work the mixture together into a dough. When you have made a ball of dough that is not too dry or too sticky (if so add more flour) then take it out of the bowl and set it on a floured surface. Now for the secret of good bread :

Kneading. To knead you push the dough away from you with the bottom part of the palm of your hand, gather it up and repeat. Soon the dough will seem elastic and evenly textured. Knead a bit more and shape into a loaf shape. You can bake the bread in any small container but a loaf tin is ideal. Grease a tin and set the bread in it. Now it's time for:

Rising. The dough must be left in a warm but not hot place. An airing cupboard is ideal, or a drawer under the stove. Cover the tin with a cloth and leave the dough to rise or 'prove' as it's known in baking circles. It should double its size in an hour. After 45 minutes turn the oven on to 450° F electricity, No. 8 gas. After an hour check on the dough and if you think it has risen enough, put it in the oven. It will be baked in 45 minutes. Using oven gloves turn it out on to a wire rack and tap the bottom. If it sounds hollow the loaf is ready. If not, put it upside down in the tin and return to the oven for 10 minutes.

A White Loaf

Follow the recipe for the Brown Loaf, but use 1 lb (400 gms) of plain white flour and 1 level teaspoon salt and 1 level teaspoon *white* sugar to feed the yeast. You will also need less water for mixing.

Soda Bread

If you have no yeast and not much time, try a loaf of Irish Soda Bread. You will need buttermilk which can be bought from most dairies. The advantage of soda bread is there's no waiting around for it to rise : the soda acts in the oven.

Oven time : 35 minutes
Oven setting : electricity 425° F, gas No. 7

1 lb (400 gms) plain flour
1 level teaspoon salt
1 level teaspoon bicarbonate
  of soda

1 level teaspoon sugar
1 small carton buttermilk

Turn on the oven.
  Sift the flour, salt and bicarbonate of soda and sugar into a large bowl. Stir in the buttermilk gradually until the dough forms a ball in the basin. You will have to judge the right amount of buttermilk from the dough. It should not be dry and cracking or sticky and damp. Place the dough on a floured surface and knead lightly. Shape it into a round cake about $1\frac{1}{2}$ ins (40 mm) thick. Grease a baking sheet and place the bread on this. With a knife cut a cross on the top. Bake it in the oven on the middle shelf for about 35 minutes and test for readiness by turning it out

on a wire rack and tapping the bottom. It should sound hollow
Soda bread does not keep well and is nicest eaten warm for tea.

If you like fruit bread, mix in a cup of sultanas or raisins into the
dough before you take it out of the mixing bowl.

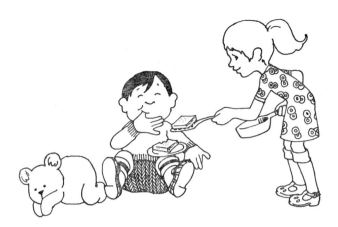

Leftovers

Risotto

Risotto uses rice to make a meal of left-over fish, meat or vegetables. You can make a simple risotto with just one ingredient, for instance mushrooms, or you can make a fancy one if the left-overs allow.

1 teacup of rice (long-grain rice, not round pudding-rice)
¾ pint (4·5 dl) stock (1 chicken or beef cube with ¾ pint [4·5 dl] boiling water poured on)
1 tablespoon oil
Salt and pepper
Your choice of left-overs (chopped ham or chicken, flaked cold fish, peas, mushrooms, cold lamb or beef)
1 onion, chopped (if you like)

Heat the oil in a deep frying-pan or saucepan. If you like onion, add it now and fry gently until the onion is transparent. Add the rice and fry, stirring all the while, until that too is transparent. Add your left-overs all chopped into small pieces. Pour on the stock and bring the mixture slowly to the boil. Add a pinch of pepper and a tiny pinch of salt. Cover the pan and simmer for about 25 minutes. Check to see if the rice is tender and the stock has been absorbed. If not cook a little longer.

Hash

This is what cowboys always eat in those old Westerns on television. I don't know when they find the time to cook the potatoes. You might have some left over from yesterday's supper.

1 small tin of corned beef
Four or five cooked potatoes
1 onion, chopped
Salt and pepper
Butter or margarine for frying

Open the tin of corned beef.
Cut the cooked potatoes into small cubes.
Heat one tablespoon of margarine or butter in a frying pan and fry the chopped onion until it begins to brown. Add the potatoes,

corned beef, and a pinch of salt and pepper to the frying pan and with a wooden spoon mix all the ingredients together. Keep mixing until the corned beef is spread evenly among the potatoes, but try not to break the potatoes up. Fry the mixture gently until it is very well heated through and the bottom has become crispy. (That is the best bit.) Professional cowboys turn it out on to a plate so the crispiness is on top.

Bubble and Squeak

I think bubble is the potatoes and squeak the cabbage or sprouts. But it might well be the other way round.

4 or 5 cooked potatoes
Left-over cabbage or sprouts
1 egg
Salt and pepper

Butter or margarine or fat for
 frying
A little flour

Put the cooked potatoes in a bowl and mash them roughly with a fork. Chop the cabbage or sprouts and add to the potato in the bowl. Break the egg into a cup and add it to the potato and cabbage. Season with a pinch of salt and pepper. Mix everything together thoroughly.

Form the mixture into small cakes with your hands. Sprinkle flour on each cake, covering them lightly all over. Heat the fat in the frying pan and fry the cakes gently until heated through and crispy on the under-side. Turn the cakes over with a fishslice and fry until crispy again. Serve them on their own or with meat or bacon or perhaps a fried egg on top.

Milk Toast

This is a remarkably good way of using up stale bread. Use it up quickly before someone turns it into bread and butter pudding.

2 slices stale bread
1 egg

Milk
Fat for frying

Cut the crusts from the slices of bread.

Pour some milk into a shallow soup plate and soak the bread. Beat the egg and pour into another dish. Lift out the bread and dip it in the egg.

Melt the fat, butter, margarine or dripping in a frying pan. Fry the slices of bread until golden on both sides. If you have a sweet tooth, sprinkle the slices with sugar while they are still warm.

A Future for Left-over Pastry

If your mother has been making pastry, ask her to give you the trimmings. Squeeze them all together with your hands and roll them out on a floured board.

Cut the pastry into squares of about 4 ins (100 mm).

In one corner of the square put your choice of filling.

You could use:

A dessertspoon of jam
Two or three slices of cheddar cheese
Some sliced apple

Slices of banana
A piece of tinned apricot or peach

Now fold over the pastry into a triangular shape. Press the edges well down. For a professional look, mark the edges with the prongs of a fork and make two small slits in the top. If the oven is being used, you can bake your 'turnovers' on a baking sheet along with whatever is being cooked. Leave them in for 25 minutes or until lightly browned.

If you want to cook them by themselves, turn the oven to electricity 375° F or gas No. 5. Cook for 25 minutes.